THROW HER DOWN

Don't Be Distracted by the Jezebel Spirit

FRANCIS A. RUNDLES, PH.D.

WESTBOW
PRESS®
A DIVISION OF THOMAS NELSON
& ZONDERVAN

WestBow Press books may be ordered through booksellers or by contacting:

WestBow Press
A Division of Thomas Nelson & Zondervan
1663 Liberty Drive
Bloomington, IN 47403
www.westbowpress.com
844-714-3454

Unless otherwise indicated, all Scripture taken from the King James Version of the Bible.

Scripture quotations marked (ESV) are from the ESV® Bible (The Holy Bible, English Standard Version®), Copyright © 2001 by Crossway, a publishing ministry of Good News Publishers. Used by permission. All rights reserved.

Scripture quotations marked (TLB) are taken from The Living Bible copyright © 1971. Used by permission of Tyndale House Publishers, Carol Stream, Illinois 60188. All rights reserved.

ISBN: 978-1-6642-4646-1 (sc)
ISBN: 978-1-6642-4647-8 (e)

Library of Congress Control Number: 2021920463

Print information available on the last page.

WestBow Press rev. date: 10/6/2021

Introduction

The spirit of Jezebel is running rampant in the world today. It is so manipulative that it is hard to recognize sometimes. It looks good on the outside because it seems to be doing great things but the inside motives are deceptive. The spirit is demonic. The goal of the spirit is to divide, conquer and destroy anything that is good because it wants to be in control and wants to make everything about them.

Dr. Francis A. Rundles, the Pastor of Greater Hope COGIC, had to deal with the spirit of Jezebel. The spirit came in and tried to divide the ministry. The spirit used some of the members to try to undermine his leadership and tried to lead some members in a different direction. The spirit of the Lord came to Dr. Rundles and gave him the Word "Too Many". The Lord let him know that everybody that is with you is not always for you. Dr. Rundles always says "it's not how many you can count but it is how many you can count on". Through the whole situation Dr. Rundles stayed prayerful, trusted and believed in Jesus, stayed in the Word of God and kept his integrity and let the Lord work the situation out for his good. The Lord assured him that the enemy would not prosper and that the ministry would stand strong because it is built on a sure foundation of the Lord.

It is so important that we understand and recognize the spirit of Jezebel. To know the true motives of people. To learn that even though that person might be doing something great are they doing it with the spirit of the Lord or the spirit of Jezebel? We must stay in the Word of God, stay prayerful and not get caught up in the world so we won't let the spirit of Jezebel get in us and use us.

Testimonials

Dr. Rundles is a rare gem. His love for God, family and the church are unmatchable. He loves everyone and his desire is for all to be saved from the wrath to come. It doesn't matter whether or not one is a member of his congregation, he will take the time out to listen and encourage you with the word of God. He takes the time to motivate other Pastors and leaders whenever they call for uplifting- for the call of God and especially the charge to Pastors, can be very draining. The encourager then needs encouraging. He often refers to the church, where he serves, as the Emergency Room. For one can come and get what they need to go out and be successful. One of his motto's is that "We are going to win the city" all for the upbuilding of God's kingdom. He is a visionary, standing as a soldier for God, praying for the next assignment so that God might be glorified through his life. One will do himself well to read this book and to help equip himself in ministry.

– Lillie Rundles

While some may refer to their pastor as a leader, preacher, teacher, or spiritual counselor. Dr. Francis Rundles can be referred to as not only a pastor, but a leader, a mentor, and a friend. Referencing the Kings James Version, scriptural text found in Jeremiah 3:15 states "And I will give you pastors according to mine heart, which shall feed you with knowledge and understanding." Dr. Rundles states, "everybody is somebody." This lets one know that everyone has a voice, everyone can be a part of; there are no big I's or little u's. By the examples Dr. Rundles teach, it equips, it encourages, and it prepares one for the daily challenges one may face Dr. Rundles often quotes scriptural text found in Philippians 4:13 that states "I can do all things thru Christ which strengthens me." And Dr. Rundles goes on to state "blessings come with persecutions, and persecutions with blessings." One may think that is an oxymoron but because of this kind of example, it lets one know there will be sunshine, there will be rain but you can make it thru this; it will not be like this always. Moreover, it teaches one to shift one's focus, and see beauty in the ashes; don't give up now; just hold on a little while longer. Lastly, Dr. Rundles is a man of distinction, integrity, and well known throughout the community. Because of his love for God, family, and the community, Dr. Rundles has touched the lives of many near and far and one can be certain, the best is yet to come.

– Terika Hatley

I thank God for my father! He's a humble and anointed man of God, a man after God's own heart. Without his leadership and guidance, I truly don't nowhere I would be. I look forward to this book being published because I know it's going to be a blessing to so many people!

– Sean Rundles

I praise God for Dr. Rundles. He is a genuine and humble man of God with a servant's heart. I am appreciative of the knowledge and wisdom he has poured into my life, as well as the Godly life he exemplifies.

– Chaz R. Curtis

Dr. Francis Rundles is a humble and devoted true servant of Jesus Christ. He has integrity, is a great leader, a great inspiration and a positive role model to so many people. He has a Godly spirit and when you spend any time around him you will see and feel the love he has for people. He also has a great passion for preaching and teaching the Word of God.

– James Turner

I am so proud of my Father and all the wonderful things God is doing in his life. I admire his perseverance and determination to follow God no matter what! Whether you're a seeker, a new believer, or a seasoned saint I know something in this book will help you in your life journey, I look forward to reading it.

– Toni C. Rundles

Dr. Francis Rundles and his ministry has been instrumental to me in many ways. The leadership of Dr. Rundles has taught me that leaders are called to serve. His love for God and the people of God, have impacted my ministry, I would say that Dr.

Francis Rundles is the Joshua of our day. His gifting has been a blessing to so many. Thank you, Dr. Francis Rundles, for being a faithful man of God who has a heart for God's people. Dr. Francis Rundles I salute you sir!

– Your friend, Pastor Devron Doss

Who is the one that brings fear, control, and manipulation? There is a diabolic spirit that has power to do those things because we tolerate it. People who have this spirit want to be your friend due to rejection you've experienced from those closest to you ... your friends, co-workers, and even family. This spirit convinces those around you that they are armor bearers, ready to serve and shield you from enemies. The spirit always wants you to be next to the person of authority. Solitude is being alone with God, but isolation is being alone with yourself. 1 Kings 19, we learn that Elijah found himself exhausted, wanting to be alone and ready to die. Job also found himself questioning his life and wanting to die (Job 3:11-13). Who or what could manifest such feelings? These are the effects of the Jezebel spirit. The Jezebel spirit will have you feeling depressed, lacking sleep, thinking impure sexual thoughts, having thoughts of suicide, and inexplicable and prolonged sickness. This spirit is out to steal, kill, and destroy your peace, joy, and confidence. How do you get your peace, joy, and confidence back? You must remove that person with whom the Jezebel spirit is in. Jesus tells us in Revelation 2:20 that he will remove you if you don't remove the Jezebel spirit. To recognize this spirit, we must dive into who is Jezebel and what is the spirit of Jezebel.

Who was Jezebel?

J ezebel was an actual person. Jezebel appears 1 King chapter 16, when she married Ahab king of Israel. Jezebel was the daughter of Eth Baal, the king and high priest of Baal. So, Ahab the king of Israel married he daughter of a perverse kingdom, who was raised in an atmosphere where sex was a path to power and influence. Jezebel inserted her control and manipulation through Ahab and his reign, and this led to the death of Naboth the Jezreelite. Naboth was killed by Jezebel because he would not give Ahab his vineyard, which Naboth had received from an inheritance from his father (1 King 21). Because of the death of the innocent Naboth, Elijah prophesied that Ahab and Jezebel would be judged specifically in the manner of their death. Elijah also prophesied that the dogs would lick their blood (1 King 21: 17).

What is the Spirit
of Jezebel?

The Jezebel spirit is born of witchcraft and rebellion. This demon is one of the most common spirits in operation today, both in the church and in the world, which is a powerful enemy of the body of Christ. She operates freely on sincere believers whose hearts are for God individually, and has also attained positions of power as powers and principalities within the church. The spirit of Jezebel is essentially one that is controlling, working through the lust of the flesh, the lust of the eyes, and the pride of life. It has in general two aims: to gain identity, glory, recognition, and power; and satisfy the need for the "Praise of Men". This is a consequence of the desire for love and self-worth focused on self.

This spirit is a man hater, in that it fosters a distrust and hatred of men in general. Jezebel spirit is in constant agitation, terribly aggressive, very determined, callous, controlling, selfish, power hungry, manipulative, unrepentant, deceitful, and overwhelmingly evil spirit (Satan's woman).

Types of Jezebel Spirits

There are two types of Jezebel spirits: one has a high profile, while the other has a low profile. The high-profile spirit is outspoken and highly visible. She is often seen as the "woman who wears the pants in the family". On the other hand, the low-profile spirit is soft spoken, gives the illusion of being motherly, protective, even appearing very submissive. The most dangerous out of the two...that would be the low-profile spirit. She is harder to discern, she relies heavily on manipulation for her power, and in extremely subtle performances is cool and a seducer.

We have discussed of the characteristics and features of this spirit, but it should be noted that the spirit is a deceiver, man-hater, unsubmitted, power-hungry, intelligent, and a hard worker. Jezebels are frequently considered "super achievers", which sadly, are admired both in the church and the business world. She is also a master in hindering and preventing others from achieving their set goals and criticizing them for not having achieved these aims. In addition to seduction, control, and manipulation, this spirit also shows characteristics of being a self-worshipper, jealousy, "queen bee" mentality, and domineering.

She uses criticism of perceived faults to build up her own self-esteem, and to justify her disobedience of or lack of respect for others. Any fault she finds in others is grounds for disobeying their authority. She uses criticism as a tool to manipulate those around her, and along with murmuring and complaints causes divisiveness to weaken her opposition and thereby gain control over and destroy them.

Bitterness and Resentment

Overcoming the effects of past hurts: (1) Inner healing=Emotional and psychological hurt linger in the form of bad memories (thoughts of hurtful experiences from the past) and barriers to personal growth. They may even lead us into various sins, emotional problems and physical illnesses. Emotional and psychological hurts including bad memories are caused both by our sin and by our being sinned against. The healing of these past hurts restores the inward or the unseen or unseeable part of men and women, as opposed to purely physical visible outward healing. Therefore, the healing of pasts hurts is commonly called inner healing. The burdens of pain that we carry drains our energy from creative and productive activity and makes us feel unworthy, guilty, hopeless, broken and unforgiveable.

Jeremiah 17:14- Heal me, O LORD, and I shall be healed; save me, and I shall be saved: for thou art my praise.

1. Make the decision to let it go. Things don't disappear on their own.
2. Express your pain… and your responsibility….
3. Stop being the victim and blaming others
4. Focus on the present- the here and now and joy

5. Forgive them- and yourself. (Matthew 6:15) & if not bitterness

Hebrews 12:15 "Root of bitterness accurately portrays the nature of bitterness. First it is hidden, when it is discovered, its noxious roots have spread and it spring up as something much bigger and more destructive."

Francis Frangipane definition of bitterness is "Unfulfilled Revenge. It is produced when Revenge is not satisfied to the degree we desire."

Bitterness and resentment against past hurts and offenses are nurtured in the victim by the Jezebel spirit because she knows a root of bitterness will grow like a cancer and manifest itself in all sorts of physical ailments, which she uses as a tool of manipulation. This inherently leads to the victim rotting from the inside out, revealing itself physically and spiritually.

What about Ahab?

The spirit of Ahab is a weak, emasculated figure. Indeed, many modern men are under the Jezebel spirit, being enslaved to their woman. If a woman plays her husband's role in directing the family, he will lose his natural drive to bear responsibility. Men who are forced in subjection to their wives tend to be angry, dejected, and retreat like Ahab. Ahab's sin and evil became progressively worse in Israel during the reign of King Ahab. Jezebel, Ahab's wife, led the way in witchcraft and idolatry so that rebellion and hardness of heart against God prevailed in Israel. In the face of such apostasy, God sent the prophet Elijah to oppose the corrupt religious system and to proclaim God's purpose for His kingdom. Jezebel persuades him to tolerate her foreign faith, then he becomes entwined in the vicious religious conflict that ends in her death.

How powerful is the demon of Jezebel?

Elijah enjoyed supernatural protection for seven years. He watched fire come down from heaven and defeated his enemies, yet when a single angry woman threatened him one time, he lost every shred of vision and ran away. He moaned in self-pity and depression begging God to kill him! Jezebel creates fear and causes men of God to withdraw. Jezebel steals our vision; Jezebel will even make us depressed and anxious when there is nothing significantly different in our circumstances.

Throw Her Down

The letter that was written to the church in Thyatira, Revelations 2:20 says, "Notwithstanding I have a few things against thee, because thou sufferest that woman Jezebel, which calleth herself a prophetess, to teach and to seduce my servants to commit fornication and to eat things sacrificed unto idols." A prevalent sin within the church in Thyatira was the tendency to tolerate sin, unrighteousness or unbiblical teaching in its leaders. Christ calls one particular person "Jezebel", a name derived from the Old Testament. Jezebel is synonymous with idolatry, sensuality, and manipulative control. People at Thyatira were submitting to or tolerating a spiritual Jezebel who exhibited great charisma, along with manipulative and seductive influence. Christ condemns this Jezebel and the freedom to sin that she represents.

We must reject, "Throw it down", all spokespersons who put their own words above Biblical revelation and who state that God accepts within the church sexual immortality and other questionable acts of compromise with the world. Some in the church may tolerate such false teaching of indifference, personal friendship, or fear confrontation because of a desire for peace, harmony, personal advancement, or money. God says He will judge such leaders and punish all those who sin in these ways and do not repent. The war continues today and what must we do? (vv 20-23; see also Luke 17:3-4).

What must we do?

The war continues today between Jezebel and Elijah, and like all wars there are casualties. Leaders sometime fall, soldiers sometime withdraw, and Jezebel wants to keep the church and the world within its present boundaries, so that she can decide the extent of the church locally. We cannot tolerate this. Revelation 2:20 reminds us that we must declare war; we will not tolerate this any longer. First, we must rid ourselves of the Jezebel way. We cannot cast out lust when we harbor lust in our lives. We cannot bring down the spirit of control if we use manipulation and hype to control our congregation. We must examine our own ways and repent of Jezebel. No compromise!

Jehu as he rides towards Jezebel to kill her, she has one more trick up her sleeves. "And when Jehu was come to Jezreel, Jezebel heard of it; and she painted her face, and tired her head, and looked out at a window," 2 Kings 9: 30. She made herself up to be in proper appearance and cast Jehu's words relative to peace. Ignoring her beauty, he asked a question, "Who is on my side? If you are on my side, throw her down and they did throw her down." We must kill every spirit that is not by God. We must recognize or identify the warning signs of the Jezebel spirit.

The Jezebel spirit's principalities are as recognized today as it was thousands of years ago. Some of the traits this spirit exhibits are that of lust, anger, murder, and the list could go on. The spirit of anger will try to get a person to act out in fits of rage and anger. The murder spirit will try to get someone to commit cold-blooded murder. The lust spirit will try to entice someone to commit fornication and/or adultery. When you come across the Jezebel spirit, it is something "different". Some people have called this a "master type" spirit. It is called this because this spirit is intelligent and more cunning than a lot of the other principalities. Simply put, a Jezebel spirit is one of Satan's top ranking, more intelligent demons. And by this demon being more cunning, intelligent, and harder to deal with, once it moves or attaches to a person, it will cause a great deal of trouble and destruction if it is not quickly caste out of a person. The Jezebel spirit likes to attach to sharp, intelligent, and very attractive people when it can. It will always seek to be the center of attention, as well as, undermine and attack anything and everything in its sight. This spirit is rebellious against leadership; it especially hates prophets, prayer, and spiritual warfare. When it comes to any form of prayer to the Lord, it knows that that our prayer life with the Lord is what keeps us in the center of His perfect will for our lives, and the Jezebel spirit will effortlessly work to destroy an individual and their prayers to the Lord.

The Bible paints a very graphic and concise portrait of this spirit, although her name is not mentioned, such as in Proverbs chapters 5 and 7. Additionally, we read in Isaiah 47:7-9, "And thou saidst, I shall be a lady forever: so that thou didst not lay these things to thy heart, neither didst remember the latter end of it. Therefore, hear now this, thou that art given to pleasures, that dwellest carelessly that sayest in thine heart, I am, and none else beside me; I shall not sit as a widow, neither shall I know the loss of children: But these two things shall come to thee in a moment in one day, the loss of children, and widowhood: they shall come upon thee in their perfection for the multitude of thy sorceries, and for the great abundance of thine enchantments." The Jezebel spirit is a principality which targets the people of God. That is both directly in themselves and indirectly through others. It can get in through uncrucified flesh and fear. Highly intelligent and devious, this seducing spirit is adept at using all sorts of manipulative tactics, especially flattery. The Jezebel spirit has the means to work against and through highly intelligent and spiritually knowledgeable people and is easily capable of carrying out completely long-term strategies. The Jezebel spirit is very evil and has been said to be like "the bride of Satan". It will often work closely with a demonic network to conceal its presence and activities, so it can be difficult to identify and break free of. The Jezebel spirit is genderless, it can take on either male, female, or any of the various forms of transgender identity including homosexual. In the scriptures it tells us that 850 males followers did her bidding. It is Jezebel-spirits of witchcraft, and religious spirits, false prophecy and false doctrine- behind the idolatry of false doctrine and cults. 850 eunuchs "ate at her table", meaning that they were fed by her food which came from the devil. "Now therefore send, and gather to me all Israel unto Mount Carmel, and the prophets of Baal four hundred and fifty and the prophets of the groves four hundred [Men], which eat at Jezebel's table," (1 Kings 18:19). Jezebel is a know it all. Quick to give his/her opinion in any area; he or she leaves little room for anyone to point out the other side of an issue. Keep in mind too, Jezebel is ambitious has strong desires, but all about self. A Jezebel leader will never say "we have a vision", but rather, "my vision is the bomb". Hosea 4:6 says, "My people are destroyed for a lack of knowledge…" Israel had broken covenant with God, worshiped other gods, and thus had changed their glory that is God into shame. The lack of a revelatory and experiential knowledge of God leads to ignorance about God's redemptive love and his spiritual principles of life, demonic deception, spiritual darkness, and ultimately destruction as the fruit of our own ways.

My observation of Jehu's Reply

How can it be peace with what your mother is doing? Joram flees for his life, but he and Ahaziah are killed. Their bodies are taken and cast in the "portion of the field of Naboth, the Jezreelite: the ground that his parent's stole." Ahab and Jezebel, the parents of King Joram, had ruthlessly defrauded Naboth to steal his field (1 King 21:1-24). Now the dead body of their son was thrown into that very field. The sins of the parents may bear fruit in their children year after the parent's death. The next set of verses in 2 Kings chapter nine is where I derived the thought "Throw her down" (2 King 9:32-37). Jezebel tried to seduce Jehu by painting her face and adorning her head and looking out of the window. In verse 32, "And he lifted up his face to the window, and said who is on my side? Who? And there looked out to him two or three eunuchs." Verse 33 says, "He said, Throw her down…" And Jezebel was killed, and thrown out the window.

The Back Story

The year was 2007 and I was awakened from a dream or vision about the Jezebel spirit. I sought out to find out about this spirit called the Jezebel spirit. There was a passage of scripture found in the Book of First Kings the 16th chapter where King Ahab marries Jezebel. Her name means "Where is the prince?" (Baal). Jezebel was the daughter of Ethbaal, the king and high priest of Baal. So, Ahab, the king of Israel, married the daughter of a perverse kingdom, who was raised in an atmosphere where sex was the path to power and influence. Jezebel was an actual person. This union with Jezebel was to bring Israel to its spiritual depths. All the ugliness and depravity of the Canaanite religious practices was now being implode in Israel.

The year was 2013 and the Lord gave me a message entitled "Throw Her Down". The message was derived from 2 Kings 9:33. We learn that when Jezebel was killed and thrown from her window, Naboth was killed by Jezebel because he would not give Ahab his vineyard, which he had received from an inheritance from his father. By giving Ahab his vineyard, it would violate the inheritance regulation of the laws of Moses (Leviticus 25:23-28; Numbers 36:7-9). Ahab and Jezebel's death fulfilled the prophecy through Jehu's slaughter of Ahab's son and the licking of Ahab's blood by dogs at the pool in Samaria.

So, in the book of second Kings the ninth chapter the prophecy of Elijah was about to pass. Years earlier Elijah had foretold the complete destruction of the descendants of Ahab (1 Kings 21:19-24). God caused the fall of the house of Ahab because it had remained stubborn and didn't repent of its idolatry and apostasy, corrupting the entire nation of Israel. Jehu is anointed King of Israel, and now rides into Jezreel to kill Joram the son of Ahab and Jezebel. King Ahaziah was killed because of his associating with Jezebel. In verse seventeen the watchmen alert them of the coming of Jehu. Joram sent out horsemen to see if he comes in peace, but the messenger returned not back to Joram, but joined with Jehu. Jehu continues towards Jezreel "driving furiously" to kill Jezebel. Joram, her son, goes out to meet him and said, "Is it peace, Jehu?" Jehu answered, "What peace so long as the idolatry of thy mother Jezebel and her witchcrafts are so many.

A Prayer Delayed is not a Prayer Denied!
What's Holding Up Your Church Blessings?

Amid the ministry growing, I found out how quick people change. Wanting to just isolate the pastor for themselves. Wanting credit and help from no one else. Always a problem affecting the special services we were having. That's when the Lord revealed unto me about the Jezebel spirit. Over the next few years, the spirit tried to undermine the vision and direction that the Lord was leading me. Rumors of secret meetings with select members of the congregation but not everyone. The spirit of God gave me to take order and set things in motion. Throw her down is a war cry for all believer to recognize this enemy and cast it out by the blood of Jesus Christ. A quote that encouraged me from the book entitled *The Bait of Satan* by John Bevere says, "Operate in your authority or else someone will and use it against you." (A wise man!) Order was restored, the ministry started to reach beyond the walls, and a separation came in the ministry. The Lord reassured me that He was with me. James 4:10 reminded me, "Humble yourself in the sight of the Lord and he will lift you up."

The Lord laid on my heart in the midst of dealing with the Jezebel spirit, the Lord gave me the thought let the sentence "play out!" What does this really mean? Play out? When a situation plays out, it unfolds and develops, and happens to perform to the end. I was told not to stop at the commas, but to go all the way to the period. So, what do I do in the middle of this situation? Hold my peace and let the Lord fight my battle. Don't try to defend yourself, sooner or later God will claim victory over this situation! In the book of Genesis 45:5, Joseph says to his brothers after they had mistreated him, "And now, do not be distressed and do not be angry with yourselves for selling me here because it was to save lives that God sent me ahead of you."

God has a purpose and a plan to expose the spirit of Jezebel. By letting the sentence play out, there will be glory for your life. This evil spirit has been responsible for not only tearing down pastors, churches, and different believers in ministry, but also it has been responsible for breaking up marriages and friendships, by tearing one another down. By allowing the sentence to play out, the person being used by this spirit will come to themselves without you intervening. To an excess, so as to be swallowed up with much sorrow; otherwise, it became them to grieve for their sin and to show godly sorrow and true repentance for it.

"Pastors and leaders must recognize, and then relinquish, any methods of control and manipulation they exercise. They must cease to gossip against fellow pastors and other believers, to talk disrespectfully about other ministries, or to reveal personal tidbits shared in confidence with them. Pastors who have privileged information, are sometimes the worst offenders of gossip. They must refrain from talebearing, before the wineskin tears."

– John Paul Jackson, Unmasking the Jezebel Spirit.

Distractions: Don't Get Distracted

The past few weeks I have been talking about distractions. What does the Bible say about distractions? Distraction is defined as a thing that prevents someone from giving full attention to someone else. An extreme agitation of the mind or emotions. The thought process is that the devil doesn't have to defeat you if he can distract you because if you lose focus you are already defeated. Luke 10:38-42 *"Now as they went on their way, Jesus entered a village. And a woman named Martha welcomed him into her house. And she had a sister called Mary, who sat the Lord's feet and listened to his teaching. But Martha was distracted with much serving. And she went up to him and said: Lord do you not care that my sister has left me to serve alone? Tell her then to help me."* But the Lord answered her, *"Martha, you are anxious and troubled about many things, but one thing is necessary. Mary has chosen the good portion, which will not*

be taken away from her." Distractions take you away from the real issues and make you anxious about things that haven't come to fruition yet. Matthew 6:34 (ESV) *"Therefore do not be anxious about tomorrow, for tomorrow will be anxious for itself. Sufficient for the day is its trouble."* Five things that distract us from God are: (1). Ourselves; Isn't it ironic that we want God, but we distract ourselves from him? (2). Work, (3). Technology, (4). Media, (5). Love and lust. Love and lust are very powerful emotions. If the enemy can't destroy you, he will try to distract you by diverting your attention away from God and putting it upon yourself. It is up to us to stay alert, so we won't fall prey to the devil our enemy. Social media has become the biggest distraction for the vast majority of people. Smartphones as well. As we can see family sitting around talking and many if not all are on their phones which causes valuable pieces of conversation to be missed by being distracted by their phones. Distractions can be anything that hinders you from perceiving or understanding what is important. The devil is always out to distract you from the purpose of the Lord. In the gospel of Matthew Chapter 14 verses 22-32 Following the miraculous feeding, which John relations in this discourse on the Bread of Life; the disciples departed across the sea of Galilee. Jesus dismissed the crowd and went up into a mountain to pray. About three miles into the lake, a great storm came up and they encountered great difficulties due to the strong winds. Between three to six a.m., Jesus came to them walking on the sea. The nearly exhausted disciples, who had been rowing all night, were thinking Jesus was a ghost. Jesus reassured them saying: *It is I.* Peter asked Jesus *"Lord if it is you then let me walk on the water.*

lower rank than the priests, they oversaw the temple worship. Unlike the priest, the Levite at least approached the victim and gazed at him. But neither extended aid. The moral of this narrative is how the lawyer was distracted because the Jews and Samaritans were bitter rivals (John 4:9). The Samaritans were despised for having a different worship center; thus, Jesus' parable was highly provocative. Samaritan was Jesus' hearers automatically a term of reproach. To portray a Samaritan as fulfilling the commandment but Jews as circumventing it would be a supreme insult to the listening lawyer and the rest of the audience. The lawyer is so distracted that he cannot even bring himself to say, "the Samaritan." Jesus shows that racial considerations are utterly transcended by God's command to love Him and thus to love Him and thus to love others as He does sisters Martha and Mary. In verse (40) the bible read that "Martha was cumbered about much serving." The word cumbered means that Martha was distracted by matters that considering Jesus the son of God's visit, should have been secondary. In verse (41) Jesus replies to her by saying, "Martha, Martha, thou art careful and troubled about many things." The repetition of her name denotes a gentle and sympathetic reply. Careful often indicates a this-worldly, unbelieving attitude that hinders proper attention to the things of God; that is, to be distracted and unduly concerned about secondary matters. The devil is the master of distraction, if he can distract you from spiritual matter with a secondary or worldly matter you will be defeated. Mary chose what was needful and that is the word of the Lord. The one thing that Jesus said refers to the spirit malnourishment craved by Mary. We must have a hunger for the things of God and not get distracted by secondary things. We must avoid being distracted by material possessions.

In the parable of the rich fool, Jesus states, "Take heed and beware of covetousness: for a man's life consisted not in the abundance of the things which he possesses. Vs. (12:15) Jesus will not be a part of furthering someone's selfish interests that are distracted by their possession. He calls for people to serve the Lord and others, not themselves. The young man was so distracted by what he had, but he forgot about what was important that is a relationship with God. Luke 12:20 "But God said unto him, Thou fool, this night thy soul shall be required of thee; then who's shall those things be, which thou hast provided?" The cares and anxiety of this life can distract us from the purpose of life. Jesus now deals with the equally dangerous tendency of those who have few possessions: worry! Which is a great distraction. Take no thought which means "Do not be anxious." This word means to be so distracted or disturbed about material needs that we distrust God and are distracted from faithfully doing His will. Anxious care is the direct opposite of faith. The question from this text was is not life more than meat and the body more than clothes? This indicates that inner mental stability must come from the spirit of a man and not from outward physical provisions. To be distracted by material possessions or to worry about the lack of them is to live in perpetual insecurity and to deprive oneself of the spiritual blessings of God. Seek ye first the kingdom of God. The disciple's focus should be on the pledge to the king and not be distracted by everything else. The contrast between the spiritual and material is again emphasized. The believer is to seek firth the righteousness that is characteristic of God's kingdom and then all these things (material things) shall be added to him. When our priority is spiritual, God will take care of the material, for where God guides, He provides. We need not stress or worry about tomorrow for enough unto the day is the evil thereof (Matt 6:34). This means that each day has its troubles and challenges to be responsibly handled, without worrying about hypothetical problems that could arise.

There is a story of a woman in the bible who had an infirmity for eighteen years, and she was bent over and couldn't straighten up. Her disability had lasted almost two decades, she only can the ground as she walked. But this day, Jesus says to her, "Woman thou are loose from your infirmity." She was instantly healed and began to glorify God (Luke 13:13) when she came to Him. The real source of her infirmity or her physical deformity was due to an attack of the devil. Jesus delivered her from the devil's grip. This should have been a glorious occasion, but here comes the distraction. Luke 13:14 "And the ruler of the synagogue answered with indignation because Jesus had healed on the sabbath day." The ruler was so distracted about the day the healing took place, rather than the miracle that had taken place. This cripple woman had been afflicted by a demonic spirit. It is a detestable sin in Christ's eyes when a person no longer hears the sighs of suffering humanity. Jesus teaches that some people are imprisoned by sin, sickness, and death, and are in distress and great need. Today we are in great danger of becoming so distracted that we are becoming insensitive to the world's misery and suffering because of the entertainment media that reveal showing immorality and violence for the sake of pleasure. The disciples will be like their master, able to see the distresses of life and hear the groaning of creation.

As I look in the chapter is of the gospel of Luke. It is easy to get distracted by the three parables of the lost sheep, lost coin, and lost son. Many people have heard them preach separately, as though they are unrelated to each other. Distracted by the details of the three scenarios you will miss The Parable of the Lost sheep if you don't look at it in the context of the whole passage from which it comes. The answer that Jesus gives is a response to a specific situation. The Pharisee's tradition forbade them to share a meal with any they considered sinful. So, don't get distracted these three parables is one single answer given in the response to their accusation of Him by the Pharisees. These verses comprise parables that show Jesus' message to be "the Gospel for the outcast. (I.H. Marshall)! This is not only a poignant picture of God's searching love but also a rebuke of the selfish murmuring of verse 2. The Pharisees were distracted by religious points of view and by their traditions. If a woman and her neighbors delight in recovering a solitary coin, and if a shepherd takes joy in rescuing a single sheep, how much praiseworthy is the being set free from the sin of a sinner? Jesus here teaches of His concern for every individual. Chapter 15 closes with the younger son returning home and the father receiving him with love and compassion. But the older son was distracted and valued his own higher privilege and despised his brother who had squandered his portion. He thought that he was superior and thus self-righteous and was now understandably annoyed that his brother was being lavished with mercy and kindness. The older son is so distracted by what he sees, and he started to vent out his grievance: His brother is enjoying a fatted calf, while he has never had even a kid, which was much cheaper killed for him. His father reaffirms him not to be distracted, and that he is well appreciated. The whole story is a moving portrayal of a loving God's persistence in seeking out the lost. And the distraction of human deliberate desire to behave unreasonably or unacceptably. Resenting such grace which exceeds our natural understanding. We must not be distracted by what is going on in our country. Our world is increasingly dark. With many distractions through the aid of traditional news sources, online and social media, the darkness seems to be growing denser and more pervasive. The result is a climate of anger, fear, hatred, persecution, prejudice, violence, immorality, and danger. We shouldn't allow these things to distract us from the purpose of the church, that is the spirit of reconciliation. That is deep mutual healing.

The apostle Paul tells us that God has given us the spirit of reconciliation with others. This is our call to witness to those who are not yet reconciled to God through the cross. Isaiah 60:1-3 "Arise, shine, for your light has come and the glory of the Lord rises upon you. We must maintain the charge that the Lord gave to the Apostle Paul. That is to open their eyes, and to turn them from darkness to light and from the power of Satan unto God, that they may receive forgiveness of sins, and inheritance among them which are sanctified by faith that is in me. I'm reminded of testimony from Patricia Raybon how she was distracted and wanted to be angry about political bigotry, and everyday racism. When she prayed unto the Lord about this her situation, The Lord answered her and said "Smile at without taking or stressing the individual that is blocking worrisome anxiety. The first thing that is needed is to take some time to calm down. Distract yourself from the worry by walking around the yard or the block. Examine your reactions, by observing them and then letting go of the things that you are not distracted by. The Apostle Paul urges Timothy to stir upkeep in full flame the gift of God. Don't be distracted by your youth, are however that is against you. This gift that in you was given by God. With the power of God in your life, you can accomplish whatever he wills us to accomplish. Love is volitional love. A sound mind is a disciplined mind (2 Timothy 1:6-10). The testimony of our Lord refers to the gospel Paul preached. His prisoner indicates that although Paul is a prisoner in a dungeon cell in the city of Rome, he didn't get distracted from the call on his life. His train of thought is that he is God's prisoner and home is merely God's agent to put him where God wants Him. Stay focus on the task ahead and don't be distracted by the sideshows. It involves a total effort of mind, emotion, and will. Distraction can cause you to miss out on what God has promised to give you. In the 13th chapter of the book of Numbers, twelve spies were sent to the land of Canaan. The report states that the land is fruitful, the people are very strong, the cities have a great fortified wall, and to top it all up there are giants that live there, and we're like grasshoppers in their sight. The report of the spies was factual; the land was fruitful, the people were strong, the cities were walled and very great, and the giants dwelt in the land. They were so distracted by the giants, they forgot about God that promised the land to them. Only two of the spies had faith to trust God, they were Joshua and Caleb.

They said in verse 30 the land is just right for the taken. The other ten spies were giving a reason why they should not enter it. They did not want to obey God. They were persuading the people not to obey God too. Know this A negative report will never produce a positive outcome. Don't get so distracted that you forget about God. Two spies Joshua and Caleb said "Let us enter Canaan at once, we are well able to overcome it. The Lord is with us. DO not fear the people of the land." But the ten fearful spies disagreed violently. They cried out, "compared to those giants, we seemed to ourselves to be grasshoppers, and that the way we appeared to them too." That comment by them is revealing to how distractions can be devastating the giants had something that was promised to them, the promised land. We can be the biggest distraction when it comes to the promises of God. One thing that was with a low self-estimate of ourselves. The giants did not say that they were grasshoppers, they said it about themselves. In polls years ago taken in America among adults in their 20s, the question was asked; What is the basic feeling you have about life? 60 percent said that it was fear. Most people defined themselves by their problems or their possibilities. A ten-ton elephant can be stake down by a trainer with the same sizes as a baby elephant. As a baby elephant trying to tug and get away from the stakes but cannot. So, they are grown memory serves or say they cannot get away. The same thing happens to humans when we are distracted by something negative that was said and we cannot get away from it. The way to overcome the grasshopper is to remember who you are, whose you are, and where your power comes from. Who are you? You are a precious creation of almighty God, made in His image. Whose are you? If you trust in Jesus Christ as your Savior and Lord, you are an adopted child of God, having been reasoned through the sacrificial death of Jesus on the cross. Where does your power come from? It comes from the Holy Ghost planted in your heart. Paul reminds us that "For God hath not given us the spirit of fear, but of power, and love, and a sound mind. (2 Tim. 1:7). In Paul's first letter to the church in Corinth, he was appealing to them to not let cultural differences distract them. Divisions will distract us from seeing the beauty of coming together. Paul appeals to them to live together in unity. No division: the devil's job is to division and distracts us from the purpose of God in our life. The first major problem by first denouncing their factorial tendencies, than by demonstrating the quality of divine wisdom as contracted with human wisdom. Paul is deeply disturbed that the Corinthians do not seem to understand the nature of the gospel and the need for discipline and submission to the authority of Christ and Paul. Paul states to them not to be distracted by who baptized you. 1 Corinthians 1:17 "For Christ sent me not to baptize, but to preach the gospel." We must keep the main thing the main thing by staying focused and not being distracted. 1:17 "Lest the cross of Christ should be made of no effect, "to empty of substance" or make of no effect: The success of the gospel lies in the plain doctrine of a crucified Lord. Don't be distracted this truth needs no artificial dress. It alone carries with it the "power of God unto salvation" (Rom. 1:16). People are distracted by cultural differences. In the gospel of John chapter 4 verse 4, Jesus states. "He must need to go through Samaria. The circuitous route (a longer route) taken by strict Jews from became more and more like the adventure of the fugitive, he gathered around him a band of rag-tag warriors. They were the offscouring of Israel. The Bible describes them as everyone who was distressed, everyone who was in debt, and everyone who was discontented. Some of the effects of being physically and mentally distracted are: *(1) you don't smile as you use too; (2) you don't love like you use to, (3) you don't get happy like you used to, (4) you don't feel the spirit like you use to, (5) you don't interact with others like you use to, (6) you don't hug like you use to, (7) you don't appreciate people like you use to, and (8) the most important one: you don't enjoy life like you use to.* Distracted by not having enough. The feeding of the five thousand is the Lord's only miracle recorded in each of the four gospels. According to John Andrew, who had brought Peter to Jesus, now brings a boy's lunch which consisted merely of five loaves, and two fishes, small baked rolls and dried fish, an adequate lunch for a boy but hardly a crumb for the immersed crowd. The simplicity of the story and its inclusion by all four evangelists should eliminate any doubt of its historical accuracy. Don't be distracted by just having a little. Twelve baskets full of fragments remained over and above what was eaten. The collection of the fragments emphasized the adequacy and immensity of Christ's provision. Jesus says, bring you're not enough to me, and He blessed what they had. Not enough became more than enough after it was blessed by Jesus. Fragments are partly broken off, detached, or incomplete. The Lord can take your little bit and give you more than enough. He gave the disciples the command to gather up the fragments. He is speaking about people, broken people. The Lord binds up the brokenhearted (Luke 4:18) "The

Lord is nigh unto them that are of a broken heart and saveth such as be of a contrite spirit. (Psalms 34:18) "I will seek what was lost and bring back was driven away, bind up the broken, and strengthen what was sick. (Ezekiel 34:16) He is encouraging us not to be distracted by our present circumstances and miss out on the opportunity to be a blessing to others. Don't be distracted by the circumstances that are going on in your life. I believe if we're honest with ourselves, then we all can say that this year 2020 has been a trying year and has left us feeling overwhelmed! What does it mean to be overwhelmed? Overwhelmed means to be affected very strongly, to be or feel upset, it means to be devastated, distressed, and to feel oppressed. We can be so distracted, that in our hearts and mind, we can get completely overwhelmed. Distracted by circumstance make it seem like every time we turn around something else is happening. Whether it's our finances, sickness, job, family friends, etc.; whatever it may be, it can leave you in a melancholy state and feeling completely overwhelmed. Before I go any further, let's look at David and why his heart is overwhelmed, David is overwhelmed because he is on the run and is hiding out from King Saul, someone who he considered to be a friend. This caught David completely off guard because he was faithful to God and faithful in service to Saul. David was taken by this and left feeling and being overwhelmed because he was faithful to God and faithful in service to Saul. David was taken by this and left feeling and being overwhelmed because someone with who he had dined with, had fought wars with is now trying to kill him. Why was Saul trying to kill David? Saul was distracted by David's anointing and got jealous and feared means insensitivity to the demands of Christ on the Christian's life. By being so distracted by the world and its influences we are not paying attention to what time we are living in. Now is our salvation nearer: The coming of Christ to deliver us from this sinful world and the world has been delivered into the control of Satan, the prince of the power of the air. The day is a reference to the time when Christ will return and establish His reign of righteousness. Let us not be distracted, but "Let us walk honestly as in the day: not in rioting and drunkenness, not in chambering and wantonness, not in strife and envying" (Rom. 13:13). Put off the clothes that were worn in the night and put on the clothes of the day. The word of the Lord opens our understanding of the purpose that God has for us. The more we meditate on the word of God, the less likely we are to be distracted by the things surrounding us. When the word of the Lord increasing the more the kingdom of God will advance. Faith in the Lord Jesus in this time that we are living in will produce something new. Faith mixed with God's word will allow the believer to go beyond the ordinary and do the extraordinary. Don't be distracted by negative situations that are happening in the world and your life. Faith mixed with God's word produces positive results. Hold on to God's infallible truths. That means that they're incapable of error; not liable to mislead, deceive, or disappoint, incapable of error in defining doctrines touching faith or morals. "Lest Satan should get an advantage of us: for we are not ignorant of his devices." (2 Corinthians 2:11 KJV). Paul knows that Satan can and will use this incident of unforgiveness to distract and diminish the work of God in the church assembly, unless it is properly handled.

The main target of Satan's attack is the gospel. If he can bring disunity to the church, which is the agent of propagating the gospel, then he will bring also dishonor on the gospel. The church that God can best use exudes God's forgiveness and consolation.

About the Author

Francis A. Rundles, Ph.D. is very knowledgable and studious in scripture. An excellent teacher, well versed in scripture. He brings the scripture to life and makes the reader understand verse by verse. He was born Francis Antonio Rundles on January 18, 1963 to the parents of Wilbert and Nona Rundles in Mt. Pleasant, Texas.  He is the Founding Pastor of the Greater Hope Church of God in Christ, Mount Pleasant, Texas. He is currently the Superintendent of the Greater Hope Outreach District and serve as the Chairman of the Board of Superintendents for the Texas Northeast Third Jurisdiction, Church of God in Christ. He is the Secretary of the Board of Managers for Titus Regional Medical Center. He serves on the Board of Directors for the Mount Pleasant Chamber of Commerce as an Executive Board member. He will serve as Chairman of the Board for the Chamber in 2022. He will be the first African American serving in that position here in the City of Mount Pleasant.

He also serves on the Mount Pleasant Chamber of Commerce Diversity and Inclusion Committee. He has a Doctor of Divinity Degree and a Ph.D. in Philosophy from Atlantic Coast Theological Seminary. He has a Bachelor's Degree in Theology and Biblical Studies from Trinity College of the Bible. On January 19, 2020, the City of Mt. Pleasant made a proclamation for that day to be recognized as Dr. Francis A. Rundles Day. He is the proud husband of Lillie Rundles for 37 years. They have three children and seven grandchildren. He retired from the Texas Department of Transportation after 30 years of service.

Printed in the United States
by Baker & Taylor Publisher Services